Dating Sucks

But It Could Be Worse

Brian A. Parker

Dating Sucks But It Could Be Worse
Brian A. Parker
ISBN: 978-0-578-46615-6

Copyright © 2017 by Brian Parker
Cover art by Maeser Anderson

Printed in the USA

I dedicate this book to anyone who has been dumped, ghosted, cheated on, heart-broken, friend-zoned frustrated, or confused...*and yet still keeps searching for the one.* This is for you!

Prologue/Intro

When you look at the title of this book you may think, "This guy is just a sad, jilted lover." But that couldn't be further from the truth! I am about as much of a hopeless romantic as they come and I date readily in hopes of finding that special someone!

Sadly however, I've had the whole gammit happen to me during my ongoing dating life: dumped, cheated-on, friend-zoned, heart-broken, ghosted, frustrated, etc. and I'm sure that if you're reading this, you can probably say the same. I think we can both agree, it sucks.

As these things were happening to me, I started to share my dating woes with my friends and family on social media using the hashtag: #TheSearchContinues. Those posts IMMEDIATELY became my most popular (and at times controversial) posts garnering thousands of likes and comments. It was then that I realized that no matter who you are, we can all agree that dating is an integral part of the human experience and that, a lot of the time, dating sucks.

The purpose of this book is to let YOU know that

even though your love life may feel completely hopeless, it really could be worse. As a great movie once said, sometimes we have 'to laugh just to keep from weeping.'

This book is perfect for use as a bathroom reader, a coffee table book, in a waiting room, for stories around the campfire, and more! Let's help everyone to realize that even though "Dating Sucks, It Could Be Worse."

Dating Sucks
But It Could Be Worse

I thought it was going to be a silent fart and it came out louder than an air horn. I never heard from her again.

~~~

I went on a date, he took me to Wendy's and said, 'Only order from the dollar menu.'

~~~

I went out with this guy who said he was gonna take me out to dinner. The appetizer had just come and he leans over and said, "Let's exchange underwear for the rest of the evening." I just said "no thank you" and he got pissed. He called me a prude and walked out.

~~~

I once went out with a girl who spent the entire date talking about how much she hates her husband which was a surprise because *I didn't know there was a husband...*she then goes on to talk about how she did NOT want to divorce him because 'he would get stuff in the divorce!'

~~~

He leaned across me in the car to throw away a cup and his sweater got caught in my braces.

~~~

I was on a second date with a guy I met on the Internet. Boring guy, fast car. He decides to evade the police while driving 120mph on the highway, takes an exit & I end up in an upside-down 350Z, which had rolled over at 90mph into a stone wall & a telephone poll. Over a year of physical therapy. Minor nerve damage. Will never Internet date again!

~~~

A guy I knew from back home in Vegas was sitting in the same congregation I was. He ended up FB messaging me during church and we got each other's numbers and made plans to hangout later. His idea of the date was to watch Mulan...so obviously we ended up making out. It was pitch black in the room and as we were making out, I felt my nose was kinda runny and he felt it too because he asked if I needed a tissue. I just said no and played it off. But then it started getting worse, so we stopped, I went over to the bathroom, flipped the light on, looked in the mirror and saw BLOOD all over my face!!! I had a bloody nose while we were kissing and I heard him from the other room go "uhhhh...?!!?" It was a huge mess and we spent hours trying to get blood out of the couch.

~~~

I was at dinner with a guy when his phone rings. He answered it, and I hear him say, "hey babe I'm just running late..."

~~~

A guy wanted me to pin him down and force him to drink his urine...

~~~

I went on a first date with a guy I knew from high school. He was the quiet, brooding, artistic type back then, and I was hoping he still was. When we first met up, everything seemed fine—he was outfitted as a hipster and even had a good job. We spent the first hour date catching up, and then suddenly he got really serious and started taking me through his murky family health history: diabetes, cancer alcoholism, and mental illnesses of all kinds. When I asked him why he was telling me all this, he said, 'Well, if we have kids someday, it's best you know all of this now.' KIDS?! I hadn't even finished my second drink!

~~~

Throughout our first date, we decided to share some fun facts about ourselves whenever the conversation ran dry. Afterward, we went back to my place and she whispered in my ear, 'Fun fact: I'm a gymnast and don't have a gag reflex.' To which I promptly responded, 'Fun fact: I'm a virgin.

~~~

My foray into online dating wasn't exactly what I expected. Prior to this particularly horrendous date, I'd only met someone from Tinder once (he was a bouncer at a club…we played Mario Kart for two dates before calling it quits). After hearing a few success stories, I decided to give it a shot again. I figured new year, new me, right? WRONG. My Tinder date 30 minutes late.

He then proceeded to tell me about his anti-sex Catholic upbringing, his desire for a homemaking wife and his penchant for feet. I am not one to judge people for their fetishes but, correct me if I'm wrong, this defs wasn't a first…

date talking point. The date ended with a somewhat unwanted sloppy kiss and a strong desire to never see this human being again. Unfortunately, during our conversation that night I let it slip where I worked. A week later, he appeared at my place of employment…for a *job interview*. Once he got hired, I requested shift times that did not overlap with his. I kept telling my superiors this guy was trouble but no one listened. Well, eventually he got fired for harassing a client…hate to say I told you so, but…

~~~

We went to the movies. He lightly stroked my pinky with his pinky for the full 120 minutes.

~~~

He took me to Taco Bell and said I could order anything I wanted as long as it was under 5 dollars.

~~~

Ended a date with her saying 'Well, it wasn't like…Sparksville or anything but you can hang out with my friends and I.

~~~

My friend's brother came over for a home-cooked dinner. The date was awful. For starters, he smelled, I think because of dirty clothing. And when we sat on the couch chatting after dinner, he was farting inaudibly, but fragrantly. In the middle of our conversation, he received a phone call that his pot dealer may have been arrested. He was so intoxicated that he asked me to drive him to a local grocery store to meet the guy who'd called him. I did, but he went in the store and never came out! He abandoned me at the supermarket. I don't know why I went on a second date with him, but I did…on our second date, at brunch, he admitted that he had dropped acid right before our first date.

~~~

I was recently divorced and this was my first date since the split. After dinner we decided we were going to walk around the city. She says she wants to drop into this shoe store real quick. The woman then proceeds to try on shoes for 45 minutes, and I said to myself 'I guess this is my cue to leave.' I said goodbye as the woman continued to try on shoes, completely unfazed…she didn't even look up at me to say goodbye.

~~~

I had to sit through *Christmas With The Kranks* while she argued about politics in my ear and tried to convince me she could talk to ghosts.

~~~

I went on a date with a woman who was really cute and had a career as a ballet teacher. On our first date she said to me: 'I think five needles pushed through the skin on the wrist is better than an orgasm.'

~~~

I went on a date to the movies with this girl and she asked if she could bring friends. I figured she meant a double date, so I said sure! She brought nine of her friends to the date. NINE. We didn't even sit in the same row, and I never got so much as a phone call. When I ran into her later, she said that the reason she didn't call me was because I didn't talk enough.

~~~

I went on a date once with a guy who intended to study *mortuary science*. He asked me how I'd feel about taking a cold bath before sex, and then staying very still throughout.

~~~

Homecoming formal my junior year. It was my first dance ever. My date picks me up 30 minutes late, realizes he isn't wearing a tie or appropriate shoes. We stop at the store where he steals a tie and some shoes, then forgets that he never made dinner reservations. So, we end up eating a $50 meal but he forgot his credit card so I end up having to pay for both our meals. He then told me he just took ecstasy and ended up freaking out at the dance, leaves me by myself and I end up having to call a cab home. Did I mention he sat in front of me in 2 classes?

~~~

5:30p – We meet at 50s diner next to my work.

5:35p – She orders a milkshake.

5:37p – She asks me about Jesus in my life.

5:39p – "Well maybe you need to read the f***** Bible!"

5:42p – "If Gandhi did not accept the Lord Jesus Christ as our one and ONLY Savior, then he is BURNING IN HELL! AND SO WILL YOU! But the Lord can still save you."

5:44p – I put $10 on the table and simply walked out of the door. "What?! Are you just going to leave me here?"

~~~

Out on a first date. We're talking about mutual friends, neighbors, family, etc., and LOTS of the names are familiar. Long story short, I discovered that she was my second cousin. Yay, rural Kentucky.

~~~

I'm on a date with this guy and it's going pretty well until he goes, "Hey fun fact, did you know ransom payments are tax deductible?"...and then he just stared at me.

~~~

I was running late to meet someone for a second date. I dashed out of my student house and started to cross a side road. Distracted by my phone, I wasn't entirely paying attention when a delivery truck turned off without signaling, hitting me just above the knee and sending me flying. When a car hits you, your life really does flash before your eyes, and I remember having vague thoughts along the lines of 'Is this what dying feels like?' Luckily – aside from some minor-to-moderate pain, my leg seemed mostly in working order, though slightly…shaken up. The driver did his public service by checking I wasn't entirely dead, then drove off once I had moved from the road. Why the hell did I get up and walk instead of, say, going home and sitting with an ice pack on me by now entirely bruised leg? I honestly have no idea. After hobbling my way to the cinema, I ended up having to pay for both tickets, as my date – despite being much, much posher than me - had apparently drained his entire bank account that week.

~~~

On a visit to a theme park with an ex-boyfriend, we went on the swinging pirate ship ride, and halfway through, he started vomiting over everyone.

~~~

He made me drive and gave me a $3 budget for food because he had $6 in his bank account. He was 28.

~~~

He picked food out of his teeth with a used golf tee he found in the seat of his car.

~~~

I decided to meet up for coffee with a girl that I had been talking to online. We talked for 45 minutes or so — normal first date topics like family, travel, etc. She then asks, 'Where did you do your undergrad?'

Now, I have a pretty good job, but that question sets the bar pretty high for a guy who didn't go to college. She is not only assuming that I went to college but is also assuming that I am taking part in some type of post-graduate school.

When I said that I went to technical school and then straight into the workforce she looked at me as if she'd never heard of such a thing. Apparently, I didn't pass all of her minimum requirements to be considered human. After a brief pause, she broke off her shocked stare, placed her hand on her forehead in a fashion that covered her eyes, inhaled briefly and followed it by a valley-girl, 'Eew!' She took her Blackberry out of her purse and whispered to herself as she typed, 'he ... didn't ... even ... go ... to ... college ...' I then saw the left thumb hold the shift key as she deliberately pressed the exclamation point about 6 times.

She pressed a few more buttons on the phone, presumably sending this text message to her total BFF. She put the phone away, looked at me, and after taking a deep breath said, 'Well that is okay. Not everybody is capable of going to college.' She put on a fake smile followed by an awkward laugh and just stared at me awkwardly. I couldn't believe that she'd react so rudely to something and then try to act as if it didn't happen.

After staring at each other awkwardly for a few seconds, I finally broke the silence by saying, 'Wow, okay. So, yeah... I, um guess it is about time to get out of here?' I stood up and she followed me out the door. I turned and began walking down the street and she followed closely and said, 'How far away is your car?' This girl was expecting a ride!

So, I stopped and turned around and said,

'Oh, I am about a block this way. Where did you park? She replied, 'Oh, I took the bus here. I don't have a driver's license.'

Now, I am normally not a rude person. Even in that situation, I was going to just walk away and let that be that, but I just couldn't pass this opportunity up. I looked at her right in the eyes and said, 'Eew!' Pulled out my cellphone and typed, 'she ... doesn't ... even ... have ... a ... license!!!' I then put my phone away...looked up at her, smiled and said, 'That's okay! Not everybody is capable of driving a car. Lucky for you, the bus stop is right over there. I hope you don't have to wait too long!'

I wish I took a picture of the look on her face as I walked away. It was priceless.

~~~

I slept with a guy on our first date, he was on top. At first, I thought he was sweating...no big deal because I'm a trooper. Then I looked up, after a weird muffled sob, and he was crying. As I stared up into his tear-filled eyes, in horror, he stated, 'Oh my God, I'm in love with you.'

"At this point, I stated loudly, 'I have to go. My mom is calling.' Rolled him off of me, grabbed my stuff, and got dressed while walking out of his house. He called after me, sobbing in the doorway saying, 'Our signs are compatible! We fit perfectly together, even in the heavens!'

~~~

Met up with a girl from OkCupid, then in approximately this order, discovered she was:
1.) Larger than she appeared in her pictures
2.) Polyamorous
3.) A foot fetish dominatrix on craigslist who also responds to missed connections posts just to troll people

4.) Homeless

I ended up buying her some cheap Chinese grub and dropping her off at her friend's house. On the way there we almost managed to bond over video games and mind-altering substances. Almost.

~~~

I went to a restaurant with this guy. When we sat down, he grabbed a waiter and said, 'Hey, can I get a booster seat?' I thought he was kidding...but then the waiter brought over a booster seat and he sat in it the entire meal. He was a normal sized guy...

~~~

After a late dinner, my date and I decided to take advantage of our remote spot in the parking lot and started getting hot and heavy in the car. Ten minutes later, we were putting our clothes back on while being escorted out of the car by a police officer.

~~~

I asked a girl on a date. She said sure. We agreed that I'd pick her up at 4pm, then we can go go-karting at the local speed way. Unbeknownst to me, she invited 2 of her friends. Since I was a spineless 19-year-old at the time, I couldn't assert myself to tell her friend not to smoke in my car, and also that I don't want to pay for their go-karting. Ended up paying around $300 for all 4 of us to go race and my "date" had to stop at the 3rd lap because she crashed with some stranger.

~~~

She showed up for the date in her "good" pajamas. Don't know what that even means? Yeah, neither do I.

~~~

I had a blind date with a guy whose teeth were so nasty he lost two of them during dinner.

~~~

Halfway through dinner, my date decided to loudly proclaim to everyone in the bar that he was starting a fart war and would buy a drink for anyone that could out-fart him.

~~~

My worst date was back when I was in college. There were many men from all over the world school. I met one from India and after we had coffee one afternoon, he invited me back to his place. There was a huge filthy mess of dishes in the kitchen, and a mountain of dirty laundry in the bedroom. "You can start wherever you want," he said, and flicked on the TV. When I asked what the hell he meant, he replied that in

India, the women do all the cleaning, so I'd better get started. I got started all right - right out the door!

~~~

I was 45 minutes late to a first date because a kid literally got murdered for his bike along the bus route I was on. When I finally arrived, I apologized and hoped to have a bit of fun since the journey had been so long and awful. The fact someone just got murdered didn't even phase him and he asked me if I liked Disney and video games.

~~~

I was on a Tinder date. We went to a museum and everything is going great. Halfway through he starts acting all weird, twitchy, nervous and was sweating. I asked him what the hell was going on and he tells me he took ecstasy before the date.

~~~

I went on a date with this guy who had this weird thing where if he started laughing too hard, he started gagging. I was worried he was gonna throw up on me!

~~~

I went to dinner with a girl who at the end told me she was taking the leftovers home to her boyfriend.

~~~

Halfway through the meal he pulled out a small screwdriver and started cleaning his ears with it.

~~~

I was supposed to go on a one on one date with this girl Jill that I met at a party. Jill arrived at the restaurant with another couple whom she introduced as "friends from work who wanted to meet you." Surprisingly, the dinner went fairly well, Jill's friends were pretty funny, and we laughed a lot. Once the dinner was over, I said, that it was nice meeting them but we should get going if we were going to make it to the theater in time for the show. Jill and her friends got quiet and started fidgeting a bit. Finally, the woman said, "Oh, I'll ask him, you two cowards." I thought they were gonna want to come with us to the theater. I couldn't have been more wrong. The woman looked at me and continued, "We all really like you, and think you're a great guy. Jill, myself, and my husband would like to invite you over to our place for some games." I thanked them and said I'd hate for the theater tix to go to waste. Maybe another time. Jill took my hand and said, "Oh, you'll like our games better than the theater." Then she winked at me. I was really confused, until they explained that their relationship was more than friendship. Jill was their "partner" and they wanted me to join them in "swinging." I was flabbergasted. I mean, I barely knew

Jill and here she wanted me not only to sleep with her, but with her two friends, during our FIRST date!! I refused, saying I didn't know them well enough to "play" like that. I asked Jill if she still wanted to go with me to the theater, but, she said "No, I'm in the mood to 'play', so we'll just call one of our regulars." I ended up paying for dinner for three, then, going to the theater on my own. I still passed a pretty enjoyable evening, after I gave my extra ticket to a lady standing in line. She was grateful, and nice, and assured me she wasn't a swinger.

~~~

A date told me he loved the smell of bellybutton lint...

~~~

My blind date asked me if I was pregnant. When I said, "No," he asked me if I wanted to be.

~~~

I wanted to impress her by taking her to an expensive steakhouse. *After* we were seated, she told me that she was a vegetarian. She had a meal of bread and a side order of potatoes.

~~~

I liked this guy, so I asked him to go ice skating with me. The only problem was that I didn't know how to ice skate, so I kept falling. By the end of the night I had bruises all over my face and a black eye.

~~~

When we got in the car my blind date put in a mix-tape (like an actual cassette tape) of himself playing the trombone.

~~~

In the summer between my third and fourth year of university, I went on the worst date ever. After a night out, we were walking and stopped into a bagel shop for drunk food. After ordering, he said, "watch this" and proceeded to steal a package of smoked salmon from the fridge and put it in his coat. I was too scared to do anything, so I quietly waited for my food and got out of there ASAP. The rest of the awkward walk before going home was spent listening to him talk about how he and his friends always do that.

~~~

Once, I met a girl through Tinder; she was beautiful and interesting - apparently, she was a background actress. She asked to meet up at a public spot just in case I was a serial killer or something, which is fair. This is Tinder after all. By the end of the date she told me she loved me and that I was an angel sent to her by God.

~~~

He said, 'I'll let you pay for yourself so you don't feel obligated to have sex.'

~~~

At the 'goodnight kiss' part, he shut his eyes tight, began singing church hymns, gave me a high five and walked away.

~~~

In a restaurant I took off my sweater but my shirt accidentally came off too…

~~~

While kissing on the sidewalk, his mom drove by slowly and screamed 'WOO! FIRST KISS!'

~~~

One guy I was chatting with online failed to mention he DIDN'T HAVE TEETH. And after he revealed this (in person) proceeded to invite me to get food. What?

~~~

So, we finish dinner and go back into my bedroom to watch a movie. Midway through the flick, she says, 'I'm still a bit hungry — I think I'll go grab a quick bite of the leftovers.' She gets up and goes into the kitchen. I decide about 45 seconds later, as my stomach rumbles, that this sounds like a great idea.

I arrive in the kitchen to see her standing over my silverware drawer, emptying it into her purse. I was shocked — I'd never had a date try to rob me before. I asked, 'What the hell are you doing?' Her reply, 'giggle Oopsie!' I was already pissed at what I saw but the girly giggling BS answer just put me over the edge.

I walked up, looked in her bag, and saw that she'd only managed to grab some of the crappier silverware so far. At that point, I reached over to the counter and grabbed a slice of the pie. I looked her in the eyes and said, 'Don't forget your desert.' Then, while holding her gaze, I dropped the pie into her purse and smashed it up as best I could with the sides of the purse to make sure it got in there nice and good. Kicked her out, never saw her again.

~~~

For this date, I suggested we go to a local restaurant that I frequented. The manager and staff knew me, and they knew it was a blind date.

~~~

A few minutes after the waitress got our drink orders, she came back out to our table.

~~~

With a pained and serious look on her face, she said 'The manager wanted me to tell you that you left your prescription for Chlamydia medicine here last night.
Want me to go get it for you?'
It took me a second to realize what the manager, my friend, was doing and I was shocked —because I didn't have that problem or a prescription for it.
My date just stared at me like a surprised owl.
I finally was able to pick my jaw up off the floor — just as the manager came out of the kitchen, laughing his a** off.
The waitress apologized profusely, saying that he told her if she didn't play along, she'd get fired.

~~~

A guy came to a date suuuuuper high…so high that he couldn't hold a conversation. All he wanted to talk about was how he needed to 'harvest his plants.'

~~~

After dating a girl for about a month, she let me know that she had spent time in a mental institution two different times for trying to kill herself. She did not do it because she was depressed or something like that. She did it so she could enter 'The land of the dragons.' She said that she still wanted to get there some day…

~~~

I hadn't seen the guy in years, but we'd had a few dates back then and stayed friends on Facebook. I'd just been dumped so when he asked me to go for a drink, I said yes. We were only meant to be having a quick coffee but he immediately launched into a rant about how terrible his life was now. He'd lost his job, tried to 'rebrand' as a comedian, which didn't work out. Then he'd broken his leg, which got infected. There was pus he explained and he asked if I wanted to see it. Before I could respond…oh - there it is. It was rancid and smelled foul…like the rotting corpse of a dead raccoon. Then he made me go to the store with him to help him carry his groceries.

~~~

I met a girl at a conference. We didn't really connect until afterwards. We started texting and flirting. Problem was, we were in two different states. After a few weeks of talking on the phone almost every night, we decided to meet halfway between us in Las Vegas. That first night I wanted her to know just how romantic I was, so I did some research and found a secluded hill in a suburban area outside of the city. After meeting up and kissing a little bit, we drive to this hillside and I pull over, roll down the windows, put on some romantic tunes and ask her to dance. We get out of the car and dance the night away. An hour must have gone by as we were dancing and kissing under the starlit night. At one point we realized the music hadn't been playing for about 10 minutes...that's when I realized the battery of the car died. Now, I knew that with a stick shift you can push start the car and thought, "well surely the principle is the same with an automatic transmission."

Wrong. It took a while to shimmy the car back and forth until it was pointing down the hill (it was perpendicular to the hill previously). I tell her, "Ok, I'll push it the rest of the way around and you leave it in neutral...once you go down the hill about 30 feet, throw it into first gear." She agrees, hops in the driver seat and I push the car to get it going down the hill. She gets a little further than 30 feet and the whole time I'm yelling, "Throw it into gear! Throw it into gear!" Well...she DID throw it into gear and nothing happened...my date was speeding to her death down a hill with no steering and no brakes. I go sprinting after the car but naturally was unable to catch up. Thank goodness it was late at night and she didn't hit any cars as she went flying throw intersection after intersection until she FINALLY coasted to a stop. When I caught up – after I caught my breath and the initial freaking out and shaking died down - we were cracking up. A car finally came, gave us a jump and we went home.

~~~

On our first date, she texted me, "I MISS YOU so much!!!" when I went to the bathroom. I was only going number one so it wasn't like I was in there that long.

~~~

Chick asked me to go to the movies. Right before I leave my house she tells me that three of her friends were also coming. I get there and she tells me they just decided to sneak into the theater and I should do the same. I must not have been as smooth as them because we all got kicked out.

~~~

So, I met this girl on Tinder. She seemed nice enough at the time and I was sorta new to this whole Tinder thing so I must admit the red flags slipped right past me. She rocked up half drunk in a torn dress. Now I'm not one to judge people's lifestyles and I was starving so for some reason I decided to press on with the date. Bad decision. I spent the next three hours listening to her moan about her current boyfriend and how he was such a controlling guy because he wouldn't let her go out on one on one "catch ups" with guys at bars. When I finally came to my senses and told her that I didn't particularly want to be on a date with a girl who was already seeing someone…she threw her drink at me and *accused me of assaulting her*. Thankfully, the bartender had been watching the entire series of events and took my side on it. She got thrown out and I didn't go on a Tinder date for the next few months.

~~~

When I was 29, a guy told me (15 mins into a first date and with complete sincerity) that I'd better start having kids soon because I was "drying up."

~~~

A friend set me up with a guy who loved his guinea pigs so much he brought them along in a cage on the date...all eight of them. I faked an allergy to them so that he'd take me home.

~~~

A guy told me, "It's so cute that you're pursuing an education even though you're a girl."

~~~

He brought me to his house before the date because I had to meet his cats. If the cats didn't approve, it was a no-go. As soon as I saw his whole house was covered with pictures of cats, it was a no-go for me.

~~~

First date - the guy said Jesus spoke to him and told him I was the one. I 'went to the bathroom' and never returned.

~~~

My friends set me up with this super hot guy. He arrived at my house and immediately hit it off with my gay brother...

~~~

My date and I were *slow* dancing at prom and I guess he got a little "over excited" during the dance. And by the end of the song you-know-what happened and when we separated my dress was all messed up. I had to leave immediately.

~~~

I saw this cute girl on insta and that we had mutual friends. Naturally, I slide into her DM's with my go-to line. She replied with a "thank you! That's so sweet!" type message. Well a week or so later she posted something to her IG story that I responded to, then she responded, then I responded again, and her one more time. So at this point, I'm thinking I have a real shot, so I ask her out...crickets. She did not respond to that. So I let it go. No problem. A couple weeks later she posted to her story and I responded with something about how beautiful she is and she responded with a thank you and expressed how sweet I am. Here's where it goes wrong. Let me tell you something, dating is not at all like a chick flick…here's how I made that difficult discovery.

After she responded, I thought, "Well she's not avoiding me completely because she's still keeping up a bit of a dialogue, so maybe she's just the type that gets asked out all the time and wants a little extra effort. I know! I'll send some flowers to her work asking her out!"

She had it posted right there where she works so I didn't think it'd be that weird. I said in the note: "Roses are red, violets are blue, we should go out……rhyming is hard." (I was just trying to keep it light, ya know?) Then I included my name and number and that was that! Well, she blocked me…never heard from her again. Half of you reading this story are like,

"Good for her! What a creeper." The other half are like, "Dang, this guy seems fun! What's her problem? I'd love for a guy to send me flowers!" I guess she fell in the former category. *Shrug*

~~~

My date took me to hooters before the prom. Then he flirted with the busty waitress the whole time and asked her to come to prom with us since her shift was almost over.

~~~

I agree to go to brunch with this girl. And ya know, brunch is always nice...accept we didn't go to brunch. She pulled one over on me and we ended up going to church. I'm a religious guy, I respect the faith; that's great, but if you say we're gonna go to brunch, let's go to brunch.

~~~

So I'm supposed to meet this Tinder girl at a bar and I look over and she is flirting hardcore with the bouncer at the front. It turns out she was trying to do that because she was not 21. I had no idea. I decide to just wait and see how it plays out with her and the bouncer. Well, not too long after, I see her hooking up with the bouncer in the corner. From what I could tell, she didn't just get into the bar that night...

~~~

I'm on this date with this guy and halfway through dinner he starts to sell me on this pyramid scheme. I'm like, "No, I'm not interested." He was sooooo pushy about it (surprise there right?), so I decide to get up to leave but right as I stand up, the guy sprints out the door and leaves me standing there. I had to pay the bill which which was well over $100. His stupid pyramid scheme clearly isn't really paying the bills for him.

A Tinder date I went on (we're in our 30's)... he shows up to the date with his mom.

~~~

My blind date went perfectly fine. That is until his mom called me the next day to ask how things went and how he could improve.

~~~

I was going on a date with a guy from a dating app and when he came to pick me up in the car, he had about 3 inches of sand covering EVERYTHING. I stood there and he explained, "Your bio said you love the beach, so I brought it to you." He then pulled out a sun lamp and plugged it into the cigarette lighter and told me to get in. We drove around for an hour while he held the lamp on me, then he dropped me off at home. The gesture was sweet but it was probably the most awkward dates of my life.

~~~

I went out with this reaaaaally short guy and the date was fine but afterwards we went to hug when we were leaving and his face is at chest level. So, we hug and his face is in my chest but then he started motorboating in my chest...like really in there. It took me a second to pull away because I was so shocked of what was happening.

~~~

She told me that a waiter at the restaurant was her ex and she loved going there with other guys to piss him off.

~~~

The guy brought me a sign that said, "Bootylicious" and asked me if I would wear it.

~~~

My date pulled up in an old car with no passenger seat--just a hole.

~~~

I once went on a date with a guy I met online. He looked normal enough, and I agreed to go on a date with him. We met for drinks, and things were really going well. Handsome, charming, seemingly normal, so I agreed to go on another date with him. We head to a really nice steakhouse, and after appetizers and his third martini, he starts to speak baby talk to me, as in "Would you wike a wittle kissy-wissy?" Our steaks arrive and he reached across the table to cut my meat for me! I'm completely freaked out, decide I'm going to the bathroom, and he asks if I need help wiping. (I wish I was making this up.) I make it to the ladies' room, where my waitress walks in after me as I'm planning my escape route, and she says, "Um, I was just listening in on your date. Your guy has put a pacifier on your plate. Do you need to get out the back?" She winds up sneaking me through the kitchen, and I slipped her a $20 tip.

~~~

A guy took me to the Tompkins Square Park dog parade on a date, followed by brunch, where he told me about how he can't have orgasms because he's on Prozac. And oh, could I cover brunch, because he makes minimum wage.

~~~

Devin seemed sweet and romantic, and I had known him for years, so when he offered to take me out to a fancy Italian restaurant, I couldn't say no. I got all dressed up in my favorite little black ensemble and waited for him. He called and asked if I could just meet him at the restaurant. Arriving outside the restaurant, he came over laughing hysterically, and he had a friend with him. I asked him what he was doing, and he said he had been to the town bar next door drinking. Devin had no interest in actually eating dinner. He just wanted to head straight to the bar. He told me eating was "overrated." So, we're at the bar and he turns to me and says, "Hey, you know what? You f***ing disgust me." Absolutely horrified, I had no idea what to say; I just sat there stunned. "What!?"

"Lighten up, it's a line from a movie." At that moment, although I had no idea which movie he was referring to or what planet he came from, I realized, 'hey you know what?

I'm a smart, beautiful woman, and the last thing I need is some a**hole alcoholic telling me I disgust him, joking or not.'

~~~

On my first date, and my first time at a sushi place, I decided to order 13 rolls. I thought "rolls" meant individual pieces of sushi. The servers had to push two tables together just to hold them all. He was not happy about how much the bill was.

~~~

I went to a baseball game with this guy. He was like, "hey you want a drink?" I said, "sure!" So he goes over and grabs a souvenir cup out of the garbage can and says, "Here, we can get free refills with these!"

~~~

At the end of the date I went in for a hug, she ducked out of the way and gave me a high five instead.

~~~

Poop. He smelled like actual poop. Not to mention we were in a small Thai restaurant and he was speaking really loudly and using foul language. I asked him to quiet down a couple of times, but he didn't take the hint.

~~~

During our date, he told me that he'd printed photos off of my dating profile to use as a character reference in an upcoming screenplay he was working on. Before I could excuse myself, he asked me loudly about what my kinks were in bed, and eventually offered to cast me in a live theater-style sex show he was directing.

~~~

A long time ago, when people corresponded by emails more than texting, I met a nice girl who said she was new in town. We decided to go catch a movie together. About halfway through the movie, my phone starts vibrating, I check the number, don't recognize it. So I ignore it. It doesn't stop going off for 10 solid minutes. So, I excuse myself to take the call, thinking it must be important.

"'Hello?' -

"'GIVE THE PHONE TO ERICA.'

"'Excuse me? Who are you?'

"'I'M JESUS F------ CHRIST AND I WILL END YOU IF YOU DON'T GIVE HER THE PHONE.'

"'Seriously, who are you?'

Bunch of loud cursing that I don't remember I decided then to see if this girl knew who the hell was on the phone. After a few minutes, she hangs up and tells me she has to go.

"The next day I get an email with an apology, and the request to go out again. She explains that it was her ex-boyfriend from a few states away, and that he didn't take the break up and move well. And I guess he went through all her emails, got my number, and found out we were seeing a movie together.

He called all the theaters in the area and gave them my description from pictures he found online of me. He told them I had a gun. Either he didn't call the one we were at or they didn't take him seriously. I replied to her saying that I don't know if we can go out again, if this guy is going to do stuff like this. I mean, she needs to either make him back off, or call the cops. I get a reply email, not from her, but from him. He was intercepting her email. Basically, the same 'BACK OFF, SHE'S MINE!'. So, I called her, told her she needs to get this guy out of her life if she wants to date people. She didn't think it was that bad, so I told her that I wasn't comfortable going out again.

~~~

Immediately after the date, I spent 20 minutes complaining via WhatsApp about how bad the date was. I thought I was talking to my friend with the same name as my date. It was my date and not my friend.

~~~

A girl I met at a party told me that not only had she been raped by aliens, but that her psychic told her that we were a good match.

~~~

Went on a date with this gorgeous girl I've had a crush on for a while. She is thoroughly convinced that the sun revolves around the earth in a perfect circle. I would have preferred a flat-earther...

~~~

Somehow got on the topic of concealed carry weapon permits on a date with a girl, she asked if I had mine. "Yes." "Do you have your gun on you?" "No, we're drinking at a bar and there's a posted sign on the door, so...that would be a terrible idea." "Oh, I have mine!

Want to see!?" Before I could say no, I had a drunk woman pointing a Sig Sauer p238 at me. Never in my life have I moved faster out of the way than I did that night. I took it from her, field stripped it (chamber was empty, thank God.), put the pieces back in her bag, walked her home.

~~~

Went on a date with a girl and when I picked her up discovered that her father was apparently a big mafia guy. I never thought it would be possible to not at least somewhat enjoy sex with a beautiful girl… but when we did later… all I could think about is how her dad was going to kill me. It was horrible. Fortunately, she is the one who didn't respond to me reaching out… which was the biggest relief of my life.

Girl broke down and started crying in the restaurant because the abortion she secretly got when she was younger was something she always regretted. All I had asked her was how her day was going.

~~~

I once went on a date with a Jehovah's Witness drug dealer. In my defense I didn't know she was a Jehovah's Witness at the time.
And to be fair, I didn't know she was a drug dealer either.

~~~

I'm off work early, on my way to a cupcake place. A guy walking toward me flashes me a big grin, then passes by. The guy suddenly comes back and stops me. "Listen," he says, "I didn't want to regret not saying hello." He's strapping, short-haired, dark-eyed. We chat, and he asks for my number. I'm nervous about handing over my info, but he seems normal enough. So, I jot down my first name and number on a scrap of paper. Heading home. There's a message on my cell phone from the guy on the street: "Call me back." I don't. The next morning, I see several missed calls from the same guy, starting at the crack of dawn. There's a more urgent tone: "I think we have a real connection!" Calls are pouring in, from two different numbers, one private. Then come the texts: "I thought you were special, but you are SELFISH and inconsiderate." In a cold sweat now, I turn off the phone. What have I done? I turn the cell back on, and a new text awaits me.

"You are going to die ALONE. B*@ch." Off goes the phone. The next day, more diabolical calls. I'm too embarrassed to tell anyone I gave my number to a guy on the street. The texts take a new turn: "My cock is hard. I want to lick your p*ssy." Payback, I guess, for being momentarily open to a stranger.

~~~

I'm chatting with this dude and he's like, "I wanna take you to my FAVORITE breakfast spot!" I'm like, "ok, let's go!" But then we pull up to a homeless shelter...he was not homeless...if fact he had plenty of money...he was stealing from the homeless!

~~~

My first attempt at online dating led me to what was a strange courtship. When we finally met up one night, she told me she had fantasies about me raping her and pooping on her chest. I hope she has found a life mate. That guy needs to be off the streets.

~~~

At the end of a date with this girl we started making out. Things were getting hot...until she bit my arm so hard that it left mild teeth marks and a massive bruise, even through my thick pleather jacket.

~~~

I took this artsy fartsy girl to a theatre for a play. Cool, whatever. Afterwards we're walking back to my car and everything is going normal. Just making small talk. She suddenly breaks down into tears and cries about missing her ex. Anyways, I take her home to boonie-ville. It was foggy as hell so as I'm heading back home I didn't see the red light until I was running it. I hit another car and totaled both of them. (Everyone was fine).

~~~

I went out with this girl once and she was trying to be fun and mysterious, so she blindfolded me on the way to the date. So, I'm like, "ok this is going to be great!" The ride ended up being a LOT longer than I expected and I took the blindfold off and she wasn't in the car and I was in a different state! I had to take a $300 Uber home. I have NO idea what happened to her.

~~~

I go on a date with this dude and he straight off the bat told me that he had a dream about me the night before. I was like, "ooo, what was it about?" And he tells me we were making out and then he started eating sushi off my big toe. He goes wayyy into detail about how it was tuna mixed with cucumber and he like really ate it and licked my toe. The worst part about all of this is that I did end up sleeping with him anyway...nothing happened with my big toe in the bedroom but I did think about it the whole time.

~~~

I was out with this guy at a restaurant and 5 minutes in he said he wasn't feeling it. He said he would give me

$10 if we could just end the date right then. HE DIDN'T HAVE $10 DOLLARS. So, we negotiated down to $7 and I left.

~~~

This one date we were walking through the park. It was beautiful. So, we're walking along and she sees this tree and stops in her tracks starring at the tree. She then turns to me and asks, "can I meditate?" I was like "uhh, I can't stop you from meditating" so I let her meditate. She said, "Ok well you're going to make me uncomfortable if you just stand there, so can you step off to the side." So, I'm off to the side standing by this bench and she doesn't even sit, she kneels down and meditated in front of that tree for like an hour. I didn't want to be rude. So, I sat on the bench and was on my phone until she was done.

~~~

On this date, this guy decides to tell me that he can sense spirits and that he can feel the spirit of Amelia Earhart next to my liver... but don't worry because he said he can get her out.

~~~

My first date in college was with a guy named Ian. I was SO excited. I got super dressed-up and went to the campus bar to meet him. It turned out to be a different Ian than the one I thought I would be meeting. I guess I drunkenly gave my number to a random guy at a party who happened to have the same name as this cute guy in my architecture class. It was super embarrassing but I made myself stick it out with a smile until the date ended.

~~~

It was my first date ever. It was in high school and we planned to go to the football game on Friday night. I was irrationally scared that something terrible was going to happen, like farting and not being able to cover up the smell. As such, I made my best friends promise to come and sit close and take credit for any wayward flatulence. About halfway through the game, someone DID fart near us, and my best friend—how I love her!—loudly proclaimed "Excuse me, I passed gas." The fart had not originated from me, and once that boy and I became official, we all laughed about it for years.

~~~

He texted for about 80% of the dinner and spent the other 20% talking about drag queens and his cats.

~~~

I asked a girl in my college class out on a date a few years ago. We had all the details set in stone, and I showed up to find out she invited the 30 other people from the class. I had to sit through an hour and a half of the "class lunch" which she gave me credit for organizing and the whole time she acted like she didn't know I was expecting to take her on a date. Ouch.

~~~

On my fourth date with a guy my mom set me up with, we were playing pool and enjoying a couple of beers when a girl came up to our table, introduced herself, and then threw her beer on my date. The girl left, and about 30 minutes later, the police showed up and arrested him. They then took me in for questioning and asked me how long I've known him, where I was on this day, and so on. I then found out my date had set his roommate on fire and thrown him down a flight of stairs. Now he's in prison, and I never accepted another blind date invitation again.

~~~

After a bad breakup, I let my mom set me up with the son of one of her friends. I knew nothing about him other than his name and the fact that he was 16 years my senior. I like older men, so I agreed. It ended up being the shortest dinner date in history — a total of 22 minutes, mostly consisting of him making outdated pop culture references in an attempt to relate to me. Every time I tried to steer the conversation towards his interests or some kind of mutual ground, he would come out with questions like "So what's your favorite show on MTV?" and "So how about that Tom Cruise and Nicole Kidman?" (You're a little behind, buddy). I was bored to tears and couldn't wait to get out of there.

~~~

I was walking ahead of him and got into the car parked out front before he could open the door for me. He knocked on the window and yelled through the glass, "This isn't my car!"

~~~

Recently I was at the movies with a guy. He kept getting up every 10 minutes throughout the move and I thought, "wow, this guy must have a really weak bladder." I found out later from photos he posted that he was on another date at the same time with another girl in a different theater!

~~~

I went on a first date to the food court in the mall. While we're eating he calls two other girls. Chats and flirts with them literally right in front of me. Now I'm just pissed and want to go home. I told him this. He convinced me that we should at least ice skate, he already bought the tickets, yadda yadda. I'm pretty far from home and don't know anyone in the area, so I agree to go with. We skate, whatever, thank God we got there late, so we were only out there for about 30 minutes (btw, he's a sh---y skater). On the drive home, he mentions that his grandfather lives nearby and it's a special day for him, would I mind if we stopped? At this point, this date can't get any worse, so I say sure, why the hell not.

We pull into a **cemetery**. You read that correctly. A where-the-dead-people-stay cemetery. It's about 11 p.m. I'm now terrified out of my mind, frantically texting my parent where I am and what they should do if they don't hear from me soon. He pulls up to a tombstone and asks if I'd like to meet his grandpa. I politely decline. He goes out there and sits for a few minutes. He returns to the car and we drive back to my house. He tried to go in for the kiss, but I was literally saved by the dog. I rush inside and lock the door and tell my now-panicked parents the story. Later, when I told him I wasn't interested, he said this verbatim, 'Fine, you were weird anyway.'

~~~

About two years ago I divorced my wife after she cheated with a guy she met at my mother's funeral. Six months after the divorce I'm on my first date with a girl named Heidi. She wanted to stop by a local tavern that was hosting a charity benefit. We did... worst decision ever. Walk in the front door and immediately I am face to face with the guy who screwed my wife.

He and I grew up as friends but lost touch until he came to mom's funeral. He attempted to say something to me and I immediately cut him off and threatened him rather harshly. He left. I spent the next 30 minutes explaining what just happened to my date. She said I should have punched him.

~~~

I went on a first date with a girl to a Hibachi restaurant. She ordered the twin lobster tails dinner and proceeded to tell me 'My boyfriend will love this' while boxing up the 1.5 lobster tails she didn't eat.

~~~

So, I met this girl on the internet, and she seemed really nice and down-to-earth. We had a lot in common including our hobbies and politics and stuff like that, so I was thinking we might hit it off. We agree to meet up in person at a coffee place. Bear in mind that I'm not super attractive and up to this point she hasn't seen any pictures of me, instead we have pre-arranged recognition signals. She walks in the door and I spot her by her clothing instantly and start waving. She gets this sort of uncertain look on her face and walks over and says 'Sam?' and when I say yes she just says, 'Haha ... no' and walks out.

~~~

Went on a date with a phlebotomist and she kept asking to take my blood. I was terrified what she may do with it and I had to say no constantly throughout the night in fear each time.

~~~

I once talked to a girl online for some time; she was really smart, quirky, funny and pretty cute. I enjoyed the conversation and thought I was in for a treat. When I saw her for the first time I learned, she had no arms, and that was a bit of a surprise-I didn't know how to react. No judgement whatsoever, you can just imagine my surprise at that discovery!

~~~

He took me to a karaoke joint.
Serenaded me with Careless Whisper.
He was tone-deaf and couldn't read.
Then he dined and dashed and I had to
go back and pay.

~~~

I went on this date and when he
shows up, he takes one look at me
and he goes "Oh, I didn't know you
were fat." I'm 5'5", 120lbs.

~~~

I'm all set to go out with this guy and I'm
pretty excited about it. An hour before

we are supposed to meet, he texts me and said, "Sorry I can't meet you, somebody died." But that was it. He doesn't say anything else. So, I was like 'he's lying, this is BS.' So, I called him out on it. I wrote him this really snappy and kinda rude text and sent it...turns out that someone actually did die! He's a funeral director and he had to go to work. I tried to apologize. He was so cute, I never would have thought he worked in a mortuary. He never texted me back.

~~~

I was on a date with a guy at a bar and he spilled his beer bottle. I grab some napkins to start helping him clean it up and then he freaked out and said "No!" and he grabbed a straw and started slurping the beer off the bar. He was like, "that beer is too expensive to waste."

~~~

We are at this fancy restaurant and about 30 minutes in I check my phone really quick and out of the corner of my eye I see he is doing something really weird with his mouth. I was like 'what is he doing?' He had reached down his throat to trigger his gag reflex and THREW UP at the table. Then was like, "Oh I must have come down with something, I'm not feeling very well. I'd better go home." It was disgusting!

~~~

On a first date when I was a freshman in college, we had to "get some cash" before we could head to wherever we were going. He took me to a blood bank to donate plasma! We got extra cash since it was the first visit for both of us and while I was there, my bed "won" the drawing and I received an extra $10. I was so shocked by all this all I could do was sit frozen and hope it was a bad dream. I couldn't get up and leave because I was hooked to an IV! Afterwards we went through a fast food drive-thru and got some sandwiches and then a case of beer. I proceeded to feel sicker than I have ever felt before and threw up all over!

~~~

I met my date at a restaurant where he and his grandma

were waiting for me...

~~~

I had my first date in like 3 months after ending a serious relationship. She told me she's scared of sleeping with a black person (I'm a black guy) because of AIDS.

~~~

My date told me he wanted to take me to a restaurant out in a ritzy town that was pretty far from where I live. Less than a minute after I get in the dude's car, he's like, "I forgot that you lived so far out. Do you mind if we don't go to the place I suggested?" I said no, not at all. Then he says, "Good, 'cause I don't really feel like driving way out there and then bringing your ass all the way back home. I mean this is just a first date." I decided to give him the benefit of the doubt, and we went to one of my favorite restaurants. We eat and he orders two drinks. He does not pay for my meal. Then once I pay for my half and leave my tip, he puts down $20 and asks me if I have any more small bills because he doesn't want to break his other $20. I told him to ask the waitress to change his d*mn $20. We leave the restaurant, and he says, "This always happens to me when I drink rum. It makes me have to pee." We keep walking, and then I realize I'm walking by myself because he stopped to pee in the alley, right in front of me.

~~~

I go to this restaurant and we had a nice time eating. We leave the restaurant holding hands walking through the city a little bit and she starts screaming, "Cops!" and runs through the alley! I'm like, "what's going on?" So, I run with her! I hit a garbage can as I came around the corner and fell. She gets away, I get caught by the cops and they were like, "why you runnin?" I said, "I don't know why I'm running!" They said "what do you mean you don't know why you're running?" To make it worse, I lost my ID when I fell so I looked extra sketchy with no ID on me...man it was crazy.

~~~

I went out with a guy who had a degree in forensic science. At one point in the conversation he told me that he could get rid of a dead body, no questions asked, and it could never be found. He then starred at me dead serious.

~~~

I had a fun (and fairly easy) hike planned that I timed to have us at the top watching the sunset. I picked her up and she said she needed to get a spray tan so that she could impress her new coworkers at an event the next day. I sat in the car for 15 mins while she got a spray tan in her friend's garage. Afterwards she said she had to take a second to take some pics. She spent 10 minutes taking snapchat selfies and sending them to people. Then she insisted we go back to her place where she showed my Taylor Swift's new music video and told me how her dream was to be a Victoria's Secret model. I left shortly thereafter.

~~~

First, he took me to the pharmacy to show me what to use to fix my acne. Then...he asked the girl behind the counter for her number.

~~~

On my first date with a guy, he asked me if I wanted to go see a movie. When he picked me up, he said it would be cheaper to just stay in his car and watch Netflix on his iPad.

~~~

My blind date showed up missing both front teeth. "Accident?" I asked. He said, "Nope, been that way since high school." (We were in our 40's)

~~~

My date asked me for my leftover calamari to give to his mom. Later as he dropped me off, he grabbed my left boob and whispered "boob" as he got out of the car.

~~~

My friend Suzy met a guy named John on Match.com, and the two went out on what started out as a normal, delightful date. John stretched the truth slightly, telling Suzy he lived on the Upper East Side. Turns out he lived in Harlem (at least another 1/2 hour from her place in New Jersey), so there was no way she was going to do the late night trip back to Hoboken, NJ. When they got to John's apartment, they were having some wine and discussing regular topics while sitting on the couch, when suddenly John flipped out about his career. He got up, paced about the room, and muttered to himself about his career failures. Suzy, creeped out by his sudden shift in behavior, decided to turn in for the night, went to bed, and pretended to sleep. Once John thought Suzy was asleep, he downed a handle of Jack Daniels, while his ranting grew more and more disturbing. After things had finally quieted down, she noticed a strange sound coming from the corner of the bedroom. She got up and saw John in the corner of the room where all of her stuff was sitting on the floor, peeing on it. Finally, Suzy made her way home to Hoboken, NJ at 2 a.m., clutching her urine-stained belongings.

~~~

Gave our waitress all the money in my wallet to seem like a bigshot. She stopped me at the door and said, "You still owe me $7..."

~~~

He said he'd take me to a fun spot. His

fun spot a retirement home garden where he played techno music for two hours because he was their DJ.

On my first date with my now husband, we went to a local pizza place and sat on the same side of a booth because it was really busy and loud. We had a great time, but when we were waiting for our check, he let out a huge fart that I couldn't hear or smell—thank goodness—but I definitely felt the massive vibration. It was ridiculous, but, lucky for him, we both started cracking up.

~~~

A guy I met online... can't remember which

site, but he scheduled the date at a bar. A bar that didn't even serve food. He was apparently a recovering alcoholic so he only ordered cranberry juice but he failed to tell me that until after I had already ordered a glass of wine. Why on earth would you invite someone to a bar if you're an addict? It was super bizarre and on top of it he turned out to be a complete a**. He ended up leaving and wanted to walk me back to the metro and I basically said "no thanks, I'll stay here for a bit." He was shocked/offended, but finally left. When he left the bartender immediately came over and was like "holy sh** that guy was a d-bag!" took care of my tab and gave me another on the house. So, there was at least a silver lining.

~~~

During a movie, popcorn fell down

my shirt. After I picked it out he leaned in and said, 'lucky popcorn.'

~~~

After dinner, my date kissed me on the cheek and said, "Wow, your perfume smells just like my ex's."

~~~

On our first date, he said, "I love it how you just don't care about the way you look!"

~~~

I went on a date and the girl's

father sat in between us the whole movie, he said if I wanted to hold a hand it could be his.

~~~

I had a great date with good food and nice conversation. I escorted her home via taxi…or I was going to until I found out that it was her husband (who I didn't know existed) that was driving the taxi!

~~~

In high school I took a girl to the movies. When I tried to make my move to hold hands, she said, "no thanks" and moved two seats away.

~~~

I was having a lot of fun at a punk concert with a Tinder date. We were moving from gin and tonics to beer when he suddenly showed up with shots. I thought, 'Yeah, why not?' After the concert, we went to his place, did the deed, and passed out. At 3:30 A.M., I woke up with throbbing pain in my ankle and couldn't put any weight on it. I thought it was broken, maybe because someone jumped on it when we were dancing. Half-asleep and still tipsy, I hopped into his kitchen and grabbed frozen spinach. I went back to bed, laid the spinach on my ankle, and immediately fall back asleep. The next morning, there was spinach EVERYWHERE. In his sheets, all over his floor, even in the cracks of his wicker bed frame. He looked at me and just said, 'What the h*ll?' I got out of there as fast as possible, and he didn't even help me hobble down the stairs. An emergency clinic confirmed that I had fractured my foot, and I never heard from my date again.

~~~

I worked at a gym and was introduced to one of the trainers at a different location. We decided to meet up for a date after work. The whole time we were eating all he kept talking about was his "special guy friend." We then walked around the outdoor boardwalk and headed back to his car. He told me he had some great CDs he wanted to show me so I climbed in and we started listening to music. Then, he asks me if I want to see a trick. I say okay — and he pulls out his penis and begins to flex it and make it wiggle. We never spoke again.

~~~

She asked if we could make a stop

before dinner. I was cool with that. It ended up being a drug deal. And then she tagged the wall of the Costco where the deal went down.

~~~

I turned down his offer to have sex at the end of the night so he took care of business right in front of me...His name was Jack...I'm not kidding.

~~~

He asked me when and how I broke my nose. I've never had a broken nose before...

~~~

One time my date told me he had to keep his phone out because his ex could be going into labor at any time.

~~~

My prom date and I were part of a big group that all went to prom together. Before the dance we decided to get dinner at a nice steakhouse. At some point during the meal, my goofy friend lays the ketchup bottle down on the table and says, "hey let's play spin the bottle!" and he gave it a hard spin. Unfortunately, he didn't close the bottle properly and the lid flew off and sent the ketchup splattering in 360 degrees of disaster. Our clothes were all covered in ketchup stains. The girls were so upset they decided to go home and skip out on prom completely.

~~~

This guy took me out on a date to a burger place and we get french fries with our meal (obviously!) Well, he had this weird way of eating them where he would pull off the ends, then squeeze and suck the middle out and then throw the outsides away like crab shells.

~~~

I text back and forth with this guy. We ended up going out to dinner. He spent 20 minutes of dinner telling me how people should be allowed to eat penguins the same way we eat chicken...he's just going on and on. And the worst part is, before he started talking about this, I HAD

ORDERED CHICKEN. And then the food came and I was like, "I can't eat this chicken."

~~~

I went on a Tinder date with this dude. I texted him beforehand telling him I'm a vegetarian because we were trying to figure out where to go. Well of course he still took me to a steakhouse and he ORDERED ME A STEAK. He ended up eating both the steaks.

~~~

I went on an online date at a fancy restaurant. He told me that women shouldn't work, gays shouldn't be allowed to marry, ranted about how he hated his female boss and closed out the evening saying that his grandfather was a Nazi and he was proud of that fact.

~~~

I picked the movie. We arrived and he found out it was rated R. He freaked and told me he had to call his Mom to get permission to watch it. He did. She said no. Date ended. We were both 21.

~~~

I was asked out by a cute coworker who was from a neighboring town. He showed up to pick me up and came in to meet my parents. My grandma happened to be there and said, 'Eric, it's so great to see you, I just had coffee with your mom.'

"'Grandma, how do you know Eric?'

"'His mom and I are cousins." I think that made us like second cousins or something.

We went four-wheeling and hung out as friends and swore we'd never tell anyone at work that we totally dodged a bullet.

~~~

We were at the bar chatting when my date informs me that she was a witch, and that she had made her last boyfriend love her by casting a spell on him. She was even nice enough to tell me how the spell works. She took a vial of her period blood and poured it into his wine and tricked him into drinking it. "Now he's mine forever" she told me. She went on to say that it turned out she didn't really love him, but because of her spell, he would love her forever. She claimed he was still desperately in love with her even though she had dumped him.

~~~

My blind date had been racking up major points throwing in French throughout the night (I don't speak it). We hit it off, but I declined when he asked me to come home with him at the end of the night. He said something in French in response but wouldn't translate. It wasn't until after our second date that I found out the translation of the word — turns out, he had called me a whore!

~~~

I went on a double date to the movies...with her parents...who sat between us.

~~~

On a first date he took me to his cousin's kindergarten graduation and then to a family party. He didn't even talk to me for the entire four hours. I was stuck there. At least there was cake.

~~~

This was during the spring, someone wanted to meet in the park. I thought that would be very nice, so we go. He excused himself to use the restroom and uses the porta-potty at the park. He was in there for a while...to the point I started getting nervous for him because he was in there so long. So, I went to go check on him, just to make sure he hadn't passed out in there or anything and as I was up to the porta-potty I could hear that he was inside watching some pretty hardcore porn. So, I just left. Porn in a porta-potty...a porn-apotty...who knew.

~~~

I went on a date with a dude and he told me, "Oh you know what, you're so gorgeous that you could be in a beauty pageant." I thought that was so sweet. He then takes out his phone to show me the specific pageant he was thinking of and that pageant was "Miss Plus Size." That is the one time I've ever slapped somebody in the face.

~~~

I ran into my ex on the street when I was out with a Tinder date one time and after we chatted with him, the charming gentleman I was with told me he was genuinely surprised I dated someone so attractive.

~~~

Back in high school I was dating a girl I met at summer camp. We went to different schools in different parts of the country, but for prom she still wanted me to be her date. So, I skyped into her prom night the whole evening. Her friends passed around a laptop with my grainy face on it while I sat home in a tuxedo on my computer trying to convince myself this was fun.

~~~

We go to a museum and he keeps his sunglasses on the entire time. I'm like "what are you doing?" He tells me it's a government thing and he can't discuss it. Then he disappears before the date is over. I'm looking at a painting and turn around and my date is gone.

~~~

He took me to buffalo wild wings, we ordered 40 wings to split and when they got to the table, he put 4 on the plate for me and he downed the rest.

~~~

I was at a park with this guy hanging out. He gets stung with a bee on his leg and immediately he falls to the grown and is screaming and crying, like having a tantrum and asks me to call his mom. He wasn't allergic, he was just a little b*#&@.

~~~

Me and this guy had been talking for about a week and decided to hang out. We had a beer when all of the sudden he rips open his shirt and he is wearing head to toe a superman, spandex body suit which he says he wears all the time just in case. Chest hair was poking out the top and he was scrawny. He probably only weighed a 160 pounds soaking wet.

~~~

After prom we got back to my girlfriend's house and we walked in on her parents having sex in the living room.

~~~

My friend decided to set me up on a blind date with one of his girlfriend's friends. The girl she brought was my cousin...

~~~

So, I went out with this guy that before I met him, he said he was 30. When I met him, he was clearly over 50! It was sooo weird. Then later on, I found out that after me, he was dating one of my *mom's* friends.

~~~

I went on a date with this guy and I told him ahead of time that I am a strict vegan but obviously he wasn't listening to me because he took me to one of those all you can eat meat restaurants. And then afterwards he wanted to watch this like, slaughter horror movie.

~~~

I got drunk with this guy in a bar and we

went back to his place to sober up and I heard a thump and was like, "what is that?" He said that he told his kid to stay in the closet "until daddy's done."

~~~

I was on a date with a guy, the date went really well actually. So, I went back to his place because things were getting a little hotter and heavier and then he got up to go to the bathroom and when he came back, he and his twin brother, his *identical* twin brother that I didn't even know came out with him...expecting...I left immediately.

~~~

Recently a guy took me to the mall. We were window shopping, just looking around and as we were leaving he said in like this really 'cool' voice, "Look in your purse." I looked and there was a bottle of perfume in there which he had stolen 'for me' and put into my bag. I was freaked out…so I went back into the mall and put it behind the counter when no one was there hoping a staff member would put it back later.

~~~

Over dinner a girl gave me specific details about how she wanted to poison her boss. This went on for almost the entire dinner and she never said just kidding.

~~~

I had a date that started out fun and we

went back to his place and hooked up. Right after I finished, he looked at me and said, "I'm sorry we can't date anymore." I asked why and he said, "because I only date virgins."

~~~

There was this guy I went on a date with in college. We went to a fun dance with another couple and my friend and I decided we wanted to surprise the guys by going bowling. We lived in a small town with now bowling alley, so we had to drive to the next town over. When we got there the one couple got out and he said, "Can I talk to you for a minute?" He then said, "How dare you" as he glared at me. I said, "Excuse me?" He said, "how dare you bring me to such a den of iniquity!" He felt that this town was worse than Sodom and Gomorrah of the Bible (and no, we weren't even in Las Vegas). He demanded I take him home. I had to go into the bowling alley and tell the other couple that we weren't going bowling. We drove back in total silence for 30 minutes.

~~~

I once got coffee with a girl 5 minutes into the date and she just starts crying very randomly. Bawling. So, I'm scrambling like, "what's going on? are you ok?" And let me tell ya, it was loud, ugly crying. People start turning their heads and she just keeps going just sitting there sobbing. Finally, she's like, "I'm so sorry, you probably don't remember this but, I treated you poorly in a past life and I just feel so bad about it."

~~~

My date was showing me his place. He opened a closet of women's clothes and said "She's moving out at the end of the month."

~~~

He printed out my online profile and handed to me when I asked what kind of people he liked.

~~~

I went to see a movie with a man I met on Tinder. Right before the lights dimmed, I noticed someone who looked vaguely familiar at the bottom of the stairs. It wasn't until he was almost at our row that I recognized him as **the guy I had been on a date with the previous week**. It was a crowded theatre, and the only seats available to him and his friends were right next to me and my date. I panicked and told my date the situation, figuring he would do something… anything. He didn't. The guy from last week's date sat right next to me and said, "well, this is awkward" as the lights dimmed.

~~~

We had a karaoke contest at my senior prom. Everybody convinced me to sing which I thought would be fine because I'm not a bad singer, but I do have terrible stage fright. When I went on stage and opened my mouth I projectile vomited on my principal and her husband.

~~~

It was my first date with a guy I met on an online personals site. We had a couple quick conversations online, but he said he wasn't a great writer so we had agreed to meet for coffee. As I sat, I imagined this really cute guy with unbelievable credentials, and was extremely excited to meet him. Finally, a guy sat down and introduced himself as my date, but instead of the 25-year-old I was expecting and was pictured on his profile, he was overweight, balding, and at least 50. He ended up talking to me for at least a half hour about how he was a 25-year-old in a 50-year-old's body, and that the picture was from his youth…

~~~

It was a blind date. He spit lasagna in my face when he laughed. I never saw him again and I still can't eat lasagna.

~~~

We went for a walk on our first date. When I tried to initiate conversation he kept saying, "please, can we walk in silence?" We got back to his house and he punched the wall on the doorstep. He then told me he loved me...

~~~

I was in a car with a guy and we are driving to the restaurant and we get pulled over by the cops. He starts to pull over and reaches to open up the glove compartment. He takes out a small bag of drugs and swallows it. I was like "What was that? Was that drugs?" He just laughed and said, "Don't worry about it." I was so nervous that I just went through with the date and still had dinner with him.

~~~

I went on a date with a guy and told him that I am a masseuse for a living. I said I am really good at what I do and charge $200 for 30 minutes. He assumed I was a prostitute and never called me back.

~~~

I was living in a new city and having met an interesting guy on a dating site. We decided to go to one of the city's many museums. I was really excited, but on my way there I realized I had gotten my museums mixed up. Instead of the quirky naturalism museum I thought I had chosen, I invited this guy to a national surgery museum. Nothing like trying to make small talk while looking through glass at formaldehyde jars with severed penises in them. Later on, it came to light that we had the same last name and it was all downhill from there.

~~~

Went out with a girl in high school and did the usual, movie and a dinner. It had been going great up until dinner, when she stumbled over a curb. I went to catch her, and promptly whacked her in the face with my head. This actually broke her nose, which lead to me panicking and trying to fix it. Of course that was a bad idea, and I think I made her nose bleed more to be honest.
Thankfully she wasn't upset at me (I spent

a good half hour freaking out over it), but there was a very awkward and at one point terrifying conversation with her dad when I brought her home. He was a former marine who served in Vietnam and did the usual 'scare the bejesus out of the daughter's date' by coming out sharpening his kabar knife when I picked her up. Needless to say, he really didn't like or trust me after that.

~~~

I once dated a girl who never worked in her life and chose not to go to college because she didn't like homework, getting up early, or having to take notes or pay attention. She said she was a writer, but never had anything published. In fact, she never even finished a story.

~~~

The worst date I ever went on was with a guy I'd known in high school. John was the captain of the basketball team, an A+ student, and all-around good guy whom I'd only admired from afar during my senior year. I saw him at a party 10 years later, and we ended up having a conversation. By the end of the evening, we had dinner plans for a few nights later. He picked me up right on time and had the reservations made — all good signs, right? WRONG! The gregarious guy from the party apparently had left on a permanent vacation, and I was suddenly sitting next to Mr. Silent. HE WOULD NOT TALK TO ME. I would try to make conversation and he would respond with, "Cool" or "Nice". Then, a couple John knew sat behind us, and he proceeded to turn completely around and have a conversation with them. He didn't even acknowledge my presence! It was horrifying. My saving grace was a friend of mine who happened to be waitressing that night. She saved me with an "emergency" phone call. John didn't even offer to drive me home when I announced I had to leave; he said "okay" and kept on talking! The best part of the story? He actually called me the next day and asked if I wanted to go out again!

~~~

On our first date he took me out for coffee where we "coincidentally" ran into his mom, so we all hung out. I was mom-bushed.

~~~

I sat down and talked to this girl for about an hour before I found out that my blind date was at a different table.

~~~

I went on a date with a vegetarian. We both ordered lasagna: mine with meat, hers without. Waiter switched them on accident. When she found out she ate meat, she stood up and yelled, "I HAVE COW IN ME!"

~~~

One time I went out on a Tinder date with this guy and he took me to this really fancy restaurant. He then ditches me and skipped out on the $150 tab. He excused himself to the bathroom and never came back. He ate all his food and left me.

~~~

I pull up at this girl's house. When I get there, she meets me outside and is all frantic and a little nervous. I thought she lived alone but when I get there, she tells me she lives with her father who wanted to meet me and she told me to act like a gay friend without telling me why. So, I play along and when I get in there, I acted extra flamboyant…I've got no problem with gay people…the whole thing was just really awkward.

~~~

I went out on a date with this guy. We were having a great time. It's going just fine. In the middle of the date he gets an urgent phone call he has to take. He comes back and tells me he has to go because his girlfriend is in

LABOR.

~~~

I met up with this date at her house. I go in and it turns out it is FILLED with pictures of some guy who turned out to be her ex-boyfriend. They were displayed everywhere as if he was famous or something.

~~~

My friends and I wanted to rent a party bus to ride to on prom. We were pumped because we got a great deal: only $50 to rent for the whole night. It turns out it was a scam. The car pulled up and it wasn't a party bus. It was an old, rundown ice cream truck with metal folding chairs in the back, but we didn't

have a plan B so we ended up riding in
the back to prom anyways.

~~~

I had lettuce stuck in my teeth and he
kept looking. I thought he wanted to kiss
me so I gave him 'the look' and kinda
leaned in. That's when he said, "you've
got spinach in your teeth."

~~~

On a blind date I found out she was
in witness protection after her ex
killed her last boyfriend and that
she had a back tattoo that said,
"love is suicide."

~~~

I was on a date with a guy who had this thing about loving to tickle people. He kept tickling me throughout the night. We went back to his place to watch a movie and he then started tickling me a lot and wouldn't stop. After 5 minutes I told him if he kept going, I was gonna pee my pants. He said, "Nuh-uh! hahaha" and kept going. I was so upset with him for tickling me nonstop, I peed my pants on purpose.

~~~

Once on a date, as a conversation starter, the guy asked me if I'd had any relatives die recently.

~~~

At the end of a first date, I asked if she'd like to go out again. She said she was going to take a break from dating for a while.

~~~

I was out with a new man I'd met. We had a great time and he suggested we go back to his house and watch a flick. So, we were talking, watching a movie and were having a glass of wine when he mentioned something about going up to get a cigarette. He slipped away and I didn't think anything of it, until 30 minutes later when I realized I was still sitting on the couch in this stranger's home. Alone. To keep from bothering him (in case he was talking to some friends or something) I texted him to ask him where he went. He texted me back 10 minutes later to tell me he was in bed. He left me, the first time in his home, alone. On the couch. For 40 minutes. And went to bed. I was so pissed I just got up, put the wine away, and walked out quietly.

~~~

I'd been asking this girl out for weeks to no avail. When she would respond, it would usually be a week or so later. One day she posts she needs help on 3 class essays. I volunteer, and she responds immediately. Over the next week, I spend about 6-8 hours helping her on (basically writing for her) all 3 essays. She got an A in the class and I never saw her again…

To make things even worse, a couple months later I asked her out to go bowling. She stood me up, but then texted me later that night to ask if we could go get fro-yo the next night…the next night came and she stood me up again…

~~~

I went on a date with a match.com chick. Ends up not looking like her pictures (of course). Halfway into dinner, she starts talking about her ex-husband. I'm actually okay with talking about past relationships so this was fine. But she then explains how he was a pedophile…and how she stayed with him for years after finding that out because she wanted to make the relationship work.

~~~

Thought we had really hit it off on the phone, when we met in person, my blind date looked nothing like he said he did and spent our entire date talking about how unattractive he is and how women constantly reject him. He also kept asking me if I thought he was ugly. I cut the date short, declined a second date, and thought I was in the clear when I didn't hear from him for a couple of days. Then, I got an e-mail from him: not a single word, just a photo of his penis.

~~~

On a blind date I took her to dinner where she popped out her fake tooth retainer and placed it next to my food.

~~~

Had a date once where halfway through dinner I noticed a piece of paper in her lap titled 'Conversation Topics.'

~~~

I was on my 4th date with this guy. At the end of the date I'm back at his place and we start making out...it turns into a heated make out session. Then he randomly he started weeping. Just bawling and crying right in the middle of our heavy making out. Turns out he was gay and he couldn't do it anymore.

~~~

I went to prom with my bf of 9 months. The dance was really fun and afterwards he drove me home. As we pulled into my house, I told him for the first time that I loved him. He responded, "Aww, I wish I felt the same." Then he got mad at me because I wouldn't make out with him after that.

~~~

We go to a movie theater. My date gets a text. He reads it during the movie and then leans over and whispers out loud that it was from his ex-girlfriend and proceeds to read the text. And then it happened five more times. Each time he read the text out loud and would giggle saying, "ha ha ha ha...can you believe her?"

~~~

When I got into the car on the first date, he said, "welcome to my lair said the spider to the fly."

~~~

I went on a date where the guy was so sunburned from golfing all day that he collapsed in the middle of dinner. I called 911 and a taxi.

~~~

It was my third week of college and I had really hit it off with this girl in one of my classes. We decided to meet up for dinner one night in the middle of the week. I got there a few minutes before she did. I greeted her and then, when she sat down she farted REALLY loud. Like unavoidably loud. She excused herself to go to the bathroom and never came back. I never heard from her again.

~~~

We'd been dating for about a year and, admittedly, I had gained bit of weight. I went over to his house to hang out, as you do when you're 17 and have zero income. After watching literally hours of him play Xbox, I was hungry (GOD FORBID). I went for a handful of cheese puffs to which he replied, "Exactly how much weight have you gained?"

~~~

I'm with this guy. He's a young, cool guy but right before the food arrives he takes out his teeth and puts in a different set of teeth! He tells me, "don't worry these are my eating teeth" and acted like it was totally normal.

~~~

I go out with this guy. We try to go for a walk. He tells me he wants to tell me something kind of serious about his life.

I thought it was a little early but was cool with it. He tells me that he was born with a "fairly long tail." Then he told me he's angry with his parents because they had it cut off when he was a baby.

~~~

He waited until after I ordered my food to tell me that he didn't want to eat...going to lunch was his idea.

~~~

I met a guy online who seemed normal (don't they all?). He requested I pick him up, which I thought was kind of odd, but I obliged...apparently, he had been day drinking (it's a Tuesday) and I had to drive. I get to the house and he tells me we need to wait so he can grab some cash from his mom first.

~~~

I got invited to a party as a second date. I thought she was really cute and our first date went well so I was excited for this second date. Girl met me at the door and walked me to where the band was playing, she then walked away with some guy. I didn't see her for a good hour before I decided to leave. Turns out he had some cocaine and she banged him to score some.

~~~

I met a girl in a college class and noticed she was looking at golf clubs on eBay. Being a golfer myself, I figured it was a perfect conversation starter and went with it. After an exchange of numbers and some conversation we had a golf date to play 9 holes at a local country club for the next afternoon.

So the first few holes went well but then the 7th hole happens. I'm about 230 yards from the green so I pull out my 3W. I see a pair of sandhill cranes that were about 150 yards down the fairway so I paid them no attention. I take my swing and to my surprise, the ball was a low line drive that got no more than a few feet off the ground. Further to my surprise, one of the birds was in the way of the ball. It was a direct hit to the neck and the bird went down for good.

And even further to my surprise, sandhill cranes mate for life so if one of them dies the other will sit there for hours crying for the other one. Little did I know, she loved these birds and the look on her face was horrific. She broke down in tears. We played the last two holes with maybe exchanging 10 words. Didn't hear from her again.

~~~

I ordered a steak for lunch and he tells me I shouldn't be eating steak and that I should get a salad so I don't get fat.

~~~

I went out to a movie and when it was over, I turned around and saw my date's parents and younger brother sitting behind us…

~~~

Within the first five minutes of a dinner date, he asked if I ever wanted to have kids. He said I shouldn't because I would 'pass on my bad genes to them' (I'm diabetic). He then told me that I have diabetes because of how poorly my grandparents ate (it doesn't work like that). The worst part of the date though was halfway through dinner when he told me that he spent time in jail for a felony charge.

~~~

I was set up on a blind date in high school and I went to the dude's farm. Suddenly, one of his goats started giving birth, so he ran to the barn and I followed. He proceeded to go arms deep into this goat and turned around to say, 'You want in on this?' No thanks. He then showered while I awkwardly chatted with his parents. We then went to a rodeo he participated in. He came in absolute last place and tried to make out with me in the truck his dad was driving.

~~~

My now-husband was picking me up at work. Thirty minutes prior to when he was supposed to get there, one of my coworkers started a fire in the kitchen by leaving a pizza in the microwave too long. I pulled it out of the microwave, tossed it in the sink, and ended up smelling like burnt grease. We ended up having a good time, although I found out later, I stunk to high heaven of burnt pizza.

~~~

I was on a blind date. We met for oysters and drinks, then we argued for a solid 30 minutes about brunch. Like, whether brunch is determined by the menu or the timeframe of the meal. Then he told me my job in public relations was stupid and made me pay for the date, which lasted 3 hours mainly because I'm too stubborn to walk away from an argument. When it was done, we shook hands and never spoke again.

~~~

This guy from work asked me out on a date after a few days of flirting with me out of nowhere (we worked together for like six months before he asked me out). I thought it was kind of odd that he was suddenly interested in me, but I agreed to go.

"I met him at his place and we took his car to dinner. When we came back, my windshield was smashed and two of my tires were flat. His response: "Yeah sorry. I just got out of a bad relationship.""

~~~

Went on a blind date with a friend of a friend and the first thing out of her mouth was 'Well Sarah wasn't kidding when she said you weren't tall' (Spoiler alert: I am fairly short). 5 minutes in, told me she didn't really see it going anywhere, but proceeded to order a

Grey Goose martini and a $30 appetizer for herself.

~~~

I once met this girl who seemed nice at first, completely innocent, nothing seemed to be wrong with her at all. We went on a couple dates and I started to like her. Until weird things started to occur, it began with her bragging to me that she got raped 38 times. Then told me that she turns into a werewolf every night. And then she said wanted to me bang her multiple times while she was on her period. Then she proceeded to try and get with my best friend and told him she was going to suck my blood to win his heart. Wtf.

~~~

I once went on a date with a guy and

while we were driving to dinner we got a speeding ticket. He asked me to pay for the ticket, because I was distracting him, and then took me to dinner where he made me foot the bill. After that he took me to a nightclub, where he told me all about other girls he brought there. I made him take me home and told him to forget my number.

~~~

I asked a co-worker out for dinner. I took her out that night to a nice restaurant. We had a few drinks at the restaurant. She said she wasn't feeling well. Apparently, she was on some medicine that made alcohol twice as powerful and she was a total lightweight. I offered to take her home, and she ended up puking in my brand-new car.

Plot twist: we actually ended up dating for over two years after that night.

~~~

I forgot a girl's name once…my roommate told me how he gets around the situation…so, I took her to Starbucks because they always ask what name to write on the cup.

~~~

I agreed to meet with a woman I met via an online dating platform. Once I arrived at the restaurant, we had an interesting conversation (made up of lots of oversharing on her part) that spiraled horribly out of control once she found out I was a lawyer. She ended up explaining her mom's current attempt to sue her dad for ownership of their family pet and then asked if I'd be willing to represent her brother (who was out on bail) in his upcoming trial.

~~~

I'd been talking to this guy online for a couple of weeks, and we decided to go running in Central Park. He told me he was training for a race. I wore a cute workout outfit and texted him to let him know what I was wearing so he could spot me. When he showed up, instead of sneakers and jogging clothes, he was in khakis and a button-down. He wanted to sit and talk, not run. I convinced him to walk around the park, but after half a loop, he complained about his feet and said he hated to get his clothes sweaty. As we passed a hot dog stand on our walk, he said he was thirsty. Did he pull out his wallet to pay for his water? Nope. When it became clear he expected me to pony up, the hot dog vendor shot me a look basically said, "can you believe this guy?" I paid and left my date there..

~~~

I made a joke about how I hoped he didn't 'murder me.' He took this to mean I was talking about rape and said he 'hoped I wasn't a feminist' because 'men have it much worse' and went on a literal 15-minute rant about men's rape statistics in prison. I made it clear that wasn't what I had meant at all, and wanted to see if we could change the conversation to make it through the meal. He replied that he was 'too fired up and couldn't talk about anything else.' I left before the appetizer got to the table.

~~~

For my prom, I decided to break dance on the dance floor. My back went out and they decided to call the paramedics. All the lights came on, the DJ stopped. Everyone was taking pictures and I ended up in the hospital. Nobody even came to see me in the hospital.

~~~

He asked me out. He couldn't find his money so I paid. After the movie, he asked for a ride home. The last words I heard him say were when we got back to his house and he said, "Oh, THERE'S my $20!"

~~~

The guy started off the date by bringing me two plastic frogs and a Snickers bar…I thought, "random, but ok…" but then he spent the whole date talking about his hair and the reproductive cycles of turtles. I never found out what the frogs were for.

~~~

I met this guy for coffee. We made pleasant small talk and then he adds that he always has to fart. Always. I didn't say anything so he goes, "Actually, I need to fart right now" and lets one loose. I could hear it over the din of the coffee shop. I said I had a family dinner and left.

~~~

I was 25 and working at a restaurant in a busy mall. There was a guy who worked at the art store next door to us who asked me out. We went to a nice restaurant and had just ordered when he leaned over the table and said, "I shave my balls." I excused myself, went through the kitchen and straight out the back door to a bar to use the phone to call my friend to pick me up.

~~~

I went out to dinner with this guy. He picks me up. We're driving there and all along the way he's pointing places out to me that he recognizes because he banged other girls there. "Yeah that apartment over there. The back of that restaurant. In a car over at that park."

~~~

After our date, we had gone back to his place so I could sober up a bit before heading back to mine. We had literally just walked in the front door when we heard a loud thud. We looked at each other and looked out the window to see what that was. A man had just been hit by a car. I ran, without thinking, to the man in the street while my date called 911. By the end of the night my heels were coated in blood, my hair was a mess (it was sleeting), and my pant legs were soaked.

~~~

My date revealed his prized tattoo to me within the first 10 minutes. It was a cartoon of him drinking a 40 oz beer.

~~~

The other day I was talking to my wife about a TERRIBLE date I went on with some random chick a few years ago. I was going on about how weird it was. I'd forgotten that the date was *her*.

~~~

I went on a Tinder date and had a good time. He was a totally normal guy. He offered to drive me home and I figured why not? We get in his car...and as we drove, he knew EXACTLY where I lived. Never asked me for directions. Never asked me for my address. Just drove me home like he'd been there a million times...

~~~

I got asked to prom by a guy I went to church with. We were just friends so I was like, "yeah"…at least I thought we were just friends. Ten minutes into the dance he asked if I would be his girlfriend and when I said "no, I think we're better as just friends" he threw his glass against the wall, it shattered, and he spent the rest of the night just quietly crying in the corner of the ballroom. He wouldn't speak to anyone and he wouldn't leave.

~~~

I was setup on a blind date. We planned to meet at a restaurant. I got there first and since it was a nice day out, I sat down on a bench outside the restaurant. He ended up calling me on his way over and I told him where I was sitting. He was still on the phone when he started walking up to the building. He took one look at me, hung up the phone and walked back to his car. I tried to call him back thinking something must have happened and he didn't answer. I received no more answers to calls or texts afterward.

~~~

I went out with this guy and we were at this restaurant. It was a nice place. We both ended up ordering a salad. When it came, he puts his fingers in the salad and starts sorting through the bowl, taking out the vegetables and lining them up on the table from "least sexy to most sexy." I sat there bewildered. FYI his least sexy was the radish and the most sexy: cherry tomatoes.

~~~

I went out with someone who drank two bottles of wine. Apparently, I slept with him anyways…I woke up in the middle of the night to find him PEEING OFF THE SIDE OF MY BED IN HIS SLEEP.

~~~

I was at dinner with a man I met online when he had a terrible choking fit that wouldn't stop. I gave him water, offered him napkins, and kept asking him if he was OK. I wanted to make sure he didn't need the Heimlich! At this point, if I were him, I would have already been in the restroom. But he was still sitting there choking, and he actually started spitting food up onto both of our plates. He finally stopped and drank some water, then he just started to eat again! He explained the choking by saying he'd eaten part of his napkin. How does that happen? I was horrified. I powered through dinner, and when we walked out, he tried to kiss me. I gagged and left...

~~~

A guy invites me over to his place for dinner and then said to me half way through that he wasn't sure if this was gonna work out and had to consult his cat about it. He walked out, was gone for about 5 minutes, came back and said the cat wasn't feeling it and that I had to leave.

~~~

My date picked me up for homecoming and gave me a corsage that his mother made from her garden. I thought that was kind of weird but also sweet. He puts it on me and we go to the dance.

While we're dancing I see a giant spider crawl out of the flowers and before I have time to do anything it bit me on the wrist. My wrist got so swollen I had to go to the ER.

~~~

I went to Chili's with a girl I was really interested in. We ended up back at her place watching a movie in bed. Before I could make my move, I ended up in the bathroom puking through the second half of Monsters University. There was no goodbye kiss.

~~~

I met this guy and we decide to go to Starbucks. He's really good looking and had nice hair. We're sitting there having a conversion and then he says, "hey, um, let's go to my trailer." I go, "Um, what?" And he says, "yeah, I have my travel trailer in the parking lot, let's go out there and relax for a bit." I look out the window and there's his Winnebago sitting there!

~~~

Have you ever had a person that you had ZERO interested in, but you could tell they were interested in you? The type where you wish you were interested but your personalities are just too different to the point you're actually turned off by that person? And you know what's worse than having someone you're interested in reject you? Having someone you're not interested in reject you. Because the former is just like, 'Oh dang, I shot my shot and it didn't work out.' But the latter is like, a deep shot to the pride like, 'how dare you pretend I was interested in you and then "shut me down!"' hahah!

That was my situation. We kept up a friendly dialogue though because we were colleagues. Well one day, this person texts me saying that our personalities are just too different and it just wouldn't work out. In my mind I was like, 'no duh! Where have you been??' But I responded cordially and that was that. Still stung tho. haha

~~~

I went on a date with a guy whose idea of romance was taking me to his family's church where they were trying to break the record for a hymn-singing marathon. To clarify, the standing record was four hours. I thought we were going to a drive-in movie.

~~~

On prom night my date ditched me to go to a party with the "cool" kids where they were drinking. He ditched me and I went home and when my mom asked her why I was home so early, I told her what happened. She was so upset she drove over to the party and reamed him out.

~~~

I went to dinner with this girl and the topic of kids/family came up. Then she dropped the line on me that she would never have kids with me because she didn't want to get mixed up with those (my) genes...

~~~

We were all sitting around the tables taking a break from dancing and my friend told me that she had a secret to tell me. So, I leaned over the table and my hair fell into the candle and with all the hairspray I had on it instantly caught on fire. My date tried to quickly put it out be throwing a glass of red punch on it and it went all over my white dress. I went home at 8:30 that night...

~~~

A guy I met online was so full of himself, there was no room for me at the table. He asked me if I liked his watch, then told me it was a $20,000 birthday gift to himself. He also told me he could pleasure himself better than any woman could. At one point, he even asked the elderly women sitting next to us if we made an attractive couple. They said yes. His response? 'That's right ladies, you can buy me online!' I was SO embarrassed and apologized to them.

~~~

I brought her to a diner right by our college campus. After the meal, I realized I forgot my wallet, and they didn't take the card that she had on her. We had to wait an hour for my friends on campus to walk over and pay for the meal.

~~~

I drove an hour out of my way to go to a coffee shop with this girl and she didn't look at me the entire time. After about 30 minutes of ignoring me she told me this wasn't gonna work out and left. I looked down at her phone after she said that and turns out he was swiping on Tinder during the date while drinking the coffee that I bought her.

~~~

I had the bright idea to suggest zip-lining as a first date activity, even though I had zero experience. I should have just given up when I slammed into a tree on the little practice zip line. But apparently I'm a glutton for punishment and I decided to keep going. Halfway through, I had a small panic attack and they had to come and rappel me off the platform. All this time, my date just stared at me, dumbfounded.

~~~

I was walking in the park with this guy and he kept putting his hands in his back pockets and then smelling them and I was like, "why is he doing that?" He dropped his phone and when he bent over, I looked at the back of his pants and there was a giant brown stain on the back...yeah, it's exactly what you think it is...

~~~

I was on a date with this girl who I met online. I thought she was the most incredible woman I've met in my entire life...therefore I was extremely nervous. I made the mistake of talking about my ex (I know...). Then about halfway throughout the date I had the worst stomach pains and had to run to the restroom where I had explosive diarrhea...I was in there for a while. I finally come out, sit down and the stomach starts going again. I run back to the restroom. After I come back out I sit down again and yet again the stomach starts churning. I threw money on the table and ran out of the restaurant. I was on the toilet for more than 9 hours over the course of the next 24-hour period and had to throw away my shirt and pants because they were totally ruined. I found out later...that piece of "pallet cleansing chocolate" she gave me earlier on was actually CHOCOLATE LAXATIVE!

~~~

My worst experience is that I've never been on a date.

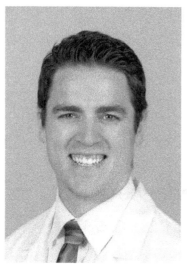

Brian A. Parker received a Bachelor's Degree in Italian and is currently a medical student. Despite the title of the book, he is a hopeless romantic. Inspired by copious horrific dating stories (of his own and others), he put together this book to help people realize that even though dating sucks, it could be worse.

To submit your stories for the next volume, please email submissions to:
datingsucksbook@gmail.com

CPSIA information can be obtained
at www.ICGtesting.com
Printed in the USA
LVHW091600110723
752161LV00005B/1063

9 780578 466156